CHEEKY

CHAT-UP
LINES

ALLSORTED.

An exclusive edition for

for all your gift books and gift stationery

This edition first published in Great Britain in 2017
by Allsorted Ltd, Watford, Herts, UK WD19 4BG

© Susanna Geoghegan Gift Publishing

Author: Roffy
Cover design: Milestone Creative
Contents layout: seagulls.net

ISBN: 978-1-910562-90-1

Printed in China

CONTENTS

INTRODUCTION

So what makes the perfect chat-up line? Humour? Charm? Cheek? The fact that it comes from the lips of George Clooney or Jennifer Lawrence?

All those things help, but not all of us are George Clooney or Jennifer Lawrence. In fact only two of us are, and let's face it, all they'd need to say is 'Hello' anyway.

Even if you're not a Hollywood A-lister, delivered with confidence and a warm smile, a simple 'Hello' may be enough to make a connection. But where's the fun in that? For those ready to proudly display their humour, charm and cheek here are over 500 more exciting ways to kick-start a conversation with the person of your dreams.

Or, in the wrong hands, over 500 strangely convoluted ways to ask for a slapped face.

INTERESTING INTERESTS

IF YOU SHARE A COMMON INTEREST
WITH THE OBJECT OF YOUR AFFECTION,
IT'S A LOT SIMPLER TO BREAK THE ICE. IT
GETS EVEN EASIER IF YOU BOTH COLLECT
ICE-PICKS, BUT THAT'S NOT A GOOD
REASON TO START HOARDING THEM.

A shared interest presents the opportunity for a targeted chat-up line. Indeed it means you can use one that would not be at all suitable anywhere else. For example, it suddenly becomes perfectly acceptable to talk to a sporty person about handling their balls.

Even seemingly unrelated interests can have a crossover. Video game fans can share with rock climbers that they both have highly developed fingers and thumbs – something that may be useful later if they really hit it off.

HOUNDS OF LOVE

BECAUSE THEY'VE HEARD ALL THE 'DOGGY-STYLE' LINES ALREADY.

- I'll be your Tramp if you'll be my Lady.

- That dog is beautiful! I see she takes after her person.

- That's a beautiful dog. Does she have a phone number?

- My dog is humping your dog – it's fate...

- Is that your dog's tail wagging, or are you just happy to see me?

- Can I sniff your bottom?

- Does your dog pee here often?

- I can be just as obedient if you want me too.

- I love to be pawed.

- You can scratch my belly.

- Fancy starting our own litter?

- Meeting you has given me a new leash of life.

- Come on, don't make me beg...

CLIMB EVERY MOUNTAIN

THE BEST WAY TO GET LEGAL HIGHS.

- You look great in a harness, want to try another one?

- You really 'rock' my world.

- Wanna get tied up and high?

- I was wondering if you could show me your favourite crag?

- See anything else you'd like to climb on top of?

- Do you like to go at it from different angles?

- Get your fleece, you've pulled.

- Please can you hold my rope and give it a tug if it gets slack?

- I've always considered bruised legs, short nails and three days without a shower really sexy.

FICTION OR NONFICTION

HOPEFULLY YOU ARE READING THIS BEFORE THE LAST LIBRARY CLOSES.

- Want to meet my book worm?

- No one believes I'm a librarian – maybe you should try to check me out.

- I'd catalogue you under 'Desirable'!

- So is it true that university librarians only let scholars in?

- I hope you're a long-term loan, because I never want to give you back.

- Charles Dickens might have given you Great Expectations, but I can meet them.

- Why don't we Middlemarch right out of here and go to dinner?

- Did I just step into an E. M. Forster novel? Because any room with you in it is A Room with a View.

- It's no wonder Big Brother's watching you. On a scale of 1 to 10, you're 1984.

- Are you an overdue book? Because you've got 'fine' written all over you.

COME OVER HERE AND LET'S GIVE THE LIBRARIAN SOMETHING TO SHUSH.

I LIKE BIG BOOKS AND I CANNOT LIE.

CALL ME ISHMAEL. WHAT CAN I CALL YOU?

19TH HOLE

MAY YOU NEVER TEE OFF ALONE AGAIN.

- Bring some friends, and we can play a foursome.
- How many strokes do you want?
- It's OK, I have two condoms just in case we get a hole in one.
- I hope you like it in the rough.
- 18 holes already today, I can barely walk.
- You look like someone who likes to swing.
- Your putt looks great in those jeans.
- I only play in the short grass.
- Want to try some new balls?

TENNIS BALLS

PUT THAT STRONG BACKHAND TO SOME USE.

- I bet I could make you grunt harder than on the tennis court.

- You've got a tight grip on that racquet. That could come in handy later.

- Tired of singles? Let's play some doubles.

- That was a pretty deep shot, but I can go deeper.

- I'd give you unlimited lets.

- You and me make a perfect match.

- You want to be my doubles partner – for life?

- Smash or pass?

- You can return my serves, but will you return my calls?

- Care to knock a few balls with me?

- Trust me, the only time I'd play games with you is on the court.

GREEN FINGERS

THE GARDEN IS WHERE THE BIRDS AND THE BEES ARE AT THEIR BEST.

- I dig you.

- Speaking of raised beds...

- I'd love to kiss those tulips.

- Are you a rosebush? Because you make me feel thorny.

- It's two green thumbs up from me.

- I was just showing this flower how beautiful you are.

- Want to help me germinate my seeds?

- What do you say to a little foraging in the woods?

- Do these plums feel ripe to you?

- If you were a flower, I would pick you.

- You make me want to get dirty.

FILM BUFF

WHAT'S ON YOUR MIND WON'T GET PAST THE CENSORS.

- Want to see the real coming attraction?

- That ticket stub won't be the only thing that gets torn up tonight.

- Can I lick the mustard off your hotdog?

- This movie isn't the only thing in the room that's feature length.

- I can think of some more fun things to do in the dark.

- Here's to a big opening weekend.

- Shall we make our own movie?

AMATEUR DRAMATICS

IT'S ONLY ONE LINE, SURELY YOU CAN REMEMBER ME.

- If you were the script I'd never want to be off-book.

- Are you a spotlight? Because you're blinding.

- Just like my last audition, you make me sweat.

- Trust me, I won't need a stunt double.

- I have the ideal part for you.

- Are you method acting? Because you're really in my head.

- You're so beautiful you make me forget my lines. Prompt!

- Would you like to star in the rest of my life?

- I have all the cue numbers written in my book, but I don't seem to have yours.

SHAKESPEAREAN STRANDS

USE TOO MANY OF THESE AND YOU WILL BE BARD.

- I'll give you my pound of flesh any day.

- By the pricking of my thumbs, something foxy this way comes.

- I'd rather compare thee to a summer's night.

- Exit, pursued by me.

- Et tu, cutie?

- Shall we make our own Winter's Tale?

- You must be part of a sonnet because I see us ending in a couplet.

- How about a little Puck?

- Is this a dagger I see before me?

- Nice Bottom.

GAME BOYS AND GAMER GIRLS

IMAGINE HOW GOOD THEY ARE WITH THEIR THUMBS.

- Mario is red. Sonic is blue. Press start to join and be my player 2.

- I've got more game than a PS4.

- I think something is wrong with my auto-aim. I can't take my eyes off you.

- Wanna leave this lobby and go into a private match?

- I usually press 'X' to pick up weapons. Does that work for picking you up as well?

- You've got a chest that I want to loot.

- I need experience points. Will you help?

- Sit on my lap and watch me 'level up'.

GYM JAMS

WHEN YOU ARE SWEATING ENOUGH ALREADY.

- Do you have any tape? Because I'm totally ripped.

- How'd you like to go on a long romantic walk on the treadmill?

- I got stopped by a police officer on the way here. He told me it was illegal to carry these guns in public.

- I know a fun activity that can burn 500 calories an hour...

- Wanna sit on my lap while I use the rowing machine?

- Let's do lunge.

- I wish this gym had a stationary bike built for two.

- Did you get those shorts in a sale? Because at my house they're 100% off.

MUSIC LOVER

WHEN YOU ARE TRYING TO ORCHESTRATE SOMETHING.

- Were you born in 1789? Because you have a classical beauty.

- Would you like to borrow my tuning fork? You're looking pretty sharp to me.

- Are you a trumpet player? Because you sure are making me horny.

- Let's make some sweet music together, honey.

- You can tickle my ivories any time you want.

- I can make you hit all the high notes.

- You had me at cello.

- Excuse me, do you believe in premarital sax?

- Would you like to play my organ?

- Flute players provide some cheap trills.

- I'd love to strum your g-string .

- I bet we'd get into some serious treble together.

EASY PC

WHEN YOUR LAPTOP STARTS TO OVERHEAT.

- You still use Internet Explorer? You must like it nice and slow.

- You know how to turn my software to hardware.

- Are you a keyboard? Because you're my type.

- If you were a browser, you'd be called FireFoxy.

- Let's bounce like a bad email.

- Are you sitting on the F5 key? Because your backside is refreshing.

- You could spam me all night and I still wouldn't unsubscribe.

- I'll show you my bits if you promise not to byte.

ON THE JOB

IF YOU KNOW WHAT SOMEONE DOES
FOR A LIVING, YOU HAVE AN OPPORTUNITY
FOR A WELL-PLACED CHAT-UP LINE.

Sometimes it's obvious. If you see someone dressed as a fireman, you know they're a fireman. Or they're on the way to a fancy dress party. Or heading to a fetish club. Thinking about it, they could be a stripper. Or just like dressing as a fireman.

Let's start again.

If you are completely, 100%, sure what someone does for a living, you have an opportunity for a well-placed chat-up line. Even better if you are in the same line of work yourself – you have your own terminology to innuendo-ise. It's amazing how easy it is to make a job sound dirty. Especially if you both farm large, male chickens.

TOTAL BANKERS

IF YOU ARE SURE YOU WANT TO BE A-LOAN WITH THEM.

- You're stimulating growth in my private sector.

- You're not an option, you're a future.

- I'm showing interest in you.

- Did I tell you I'm filthy rich and my mother's dead?

- Do you like to role play? I'll be the banking industry and you can default on your mortgage.

- Good thing I have life insurance – when I saw you my heart stopped!

- Would you be receptive to a takeover bid?

- I hope I haven't given you the wrong impression. I'm actually taller and richer than I look.

- I'll be your credit if you'll be my debit.

- Can I liquefy your assets?

- You're a hot commodity.

- You're finer than the print on my credit card statement.

DESIGNS ON DESIGNERS

CROP OUT THEIR EXISTING PARTNER FIRST.

- A portrait of you will need no photoshop at all.
- Can I select your area with my magic wand?
- First I think I'll stroke your curve, then I'd like to fill you.
- Futura generations will speak of our romance.
- I hate Comic Sans too... wanna dance?
- I like to be touched... and re-touched.
- I'm not a photographer, but I can picture us together.
- Mind if I take you for a usability test?
- Everyone else was a rough draft. You are the final copy.
- I like my fonts sans-serif, and you sans-clothes.
- You can adjust my curves any day.
- You're turning my descender into an ascender.

DO YOU HAVE A STICKING PLASTER? BECAUSE I JUST SCRAPED MY KNEE FALLING FOR YOU.

DOCTORS AND NURSES

WHERE THERE IS A PULSE THERE IS A CHANCE.

- Can I take your temperature? Because you're looking hot today.

- Can I study your anatomy?

- I'm an organ donor, need anything?

- I think you're suffering from a lack of Vitamin Me.

- I wish I was your coronary artery, so I could be wrapped around your heart.

- I'm an expert in mouth-to-mouth.

- I'm familiar with Latex and restraints.

- I'm no organ donor, but I'd be happy to give you my heart.

- Do you have an inhaler? You took my breath away.

- Playing doctor is for kids. Let's play gynaecologist!

- You have acute angina.

SILVER SERVICE

IS THAT A FLY IN YOUR SOUP?

- Since you're on your feet all day, would you like to lie down with me when you're done?

- What time do you get off? Well, what time do you get out of work?

- You brought me lunch, can I buy you dinner?

- We should get some coffee later, because I'm liking you a latte.

- Do you have any salad undressing?

- Now what's on the menu? Me-n-u.

- I'm in the mood for pizza. A pizza you, that is!

FIREFIGHTER FANCIES

ONLY FOR EMERGENCIES.

- Can I slide down your pole?

- You're so hot, a fireman couldn't put you out.

- I could make you scream louder than the siren.

- I would climb you like a ladder.

- It's true that firemen have the longest hoses.

- My job is to extinguish fires, but if you'd like to start one, call me.

- The fire might be out but you are still smoking hot.

- The hotter you get, the faster we come.

FILMMAKER FANTASIES

THE FIRST EDIT OF THIS TITLE DID NOT PLAY WELL WITH TEST AUDIENCES.

- You make my heart skip a frame.

- You are the only action I want.

- You sure make the cut.

- This chat-up line may not be the best, but we can fix it in post.

- You make me lose control of my jib.

- I'd give you extra screen time.

- Wanna find out why they call me the human tripod?

- You pull my focus.

SOLICITING SOLICITORS

WHEN YOU WANT TO START COURTING.

- Are you pro-bono or just happy to see me?

- Girl, I can sustain an objection for at least four hours.

- This is my opening statement, but it's up to you to close.

- Do you have a good lawyer? Because you just stole my heart.

- If I were on a jury I'd find you guilty of being gorgeous.

- Call me when you want to get a divorce.

- I love you beyond a reasonable doubt.

- I need someone to look through these briefs.

- I'd have to plead insanity if I ever left you.

- I'm going to sue the pants off you.

- Let's adjourn to the bedroom.

- Nice rebuttal.

- The prosecution can rest at my place tonight.

DID IT HURT
WHEN YOU
FELL FROM
HEAVEN?
BECAUSE
I KNOW
A GOOD
PERSONAL
INJURY
LAWYER.

FAVOURING THE FIGHTING FORCES

TARGET ACQUIRED, WEAPONS ARE HOT, CLEARED TO ENGAGE.

- Are you an officer? Because you make my private stand to attention.

- Can I whisky tango all over your foxtrot?

- I know how to handle a 6-inch barrel.

- I'd swab your poop deck any day.

- I can stand at attention for hours.

- I'd like to ambush your bunker.

- The penalty for being out of uniform is a spanking.

- Want to go aboard?

- Want to help me dishonourably discharge?

- I'm a drill sergeant.

GOOD COP, NAUGHTY COP

THE HELMET COMES OUT WHEN THE SITUATION IS SERIOUS.

- You have the right to remain silent. I doubt you will.

- I'm ready to enforce the law of attraction.

- I have a great idea for those handcuffs.

- I love a big bust.

- Let's go to my place for some under-cover work.

- Stick with me and those lights won't be the only thing flashing.

- Want to plant something on me?

- If being sexy was a crime, you'd be guilty as charged.

- Anything you say will be taken down. Say 'clothes'.

TRADESMEN'S ENTRANCE

SOMETHING NEEDS FIXING.

- Let's get hammered, I'll get some wood, and then I nail you.

- You are the perfect switch. You turn me on.

- I'm feeling sparks.

- My, that's a thick cable.

- Let me help you fix those shorts.

- Can I tinker with your pipes?

- That tool belt really brings out the colour in your eyes.

- I have the right tool for the job.

DENTIST DATING

YOU MAY NEED TO WASH OUT YOUR MOUTH AFTERWARDS.

- Can you feel this?

- It looks like you've got a hole that needs filling.

- Open wide.

- How far back does this chair go?

- You're so sweet I'm getting cavities.

- Your enamel is not the only thing that's hard.

- Stop undressing me with your eyes – use your teeth...

- Would you like me to teach you how to floss?

TEACHER'S PET

WHAT HAPPENS IN THE STAFFROOM, STAYS IN THE STAFFROOM.

- I've been a naughty pupil. You should teach me a lesson.

- You solve all my problems.

- I've got something better than an apple for you.

- I'll do anything to get an A.

- If you were homework I'd slam you down on my desk and do you right away.

- You've got one significant figure.

- Is there a science classroom nearby, or am I just sensing the chemistry between us?

BUSINESS AFFAIRS

YOU NEED SOMETHING TO DO BETWEEN MEETINGS.

- Time for a debrief?

- Can I expense you a drink?

- Do you have the Wi-Fi password? Because I'm feeling this connection.

- Let me be your human resource.

- Can you file a workplace safety incident report? I just fell for you.

- My account is totally receivable.

- Can I see the inside of your cubicle?

- I'd like to think inside your box.

- Want to take a look at my benefit package?

ACCOUNTANT ACCORD

RELATIONSHIPS SHOULDN'T BE TAXING.

- I'll give you an experience you won't write off anytime soon.
- You balance my books.
- You just accrued my love.
- Tell me more about double entry.
- I'm gonna have to make some adjustments to your bottom line.
- That's the largest endowment I've ever seen.
- Being with me is so good it should be taxable.
- You make me file for an extension.
- So, how do you feel about things in arrears?
- Do you want me to audit your assets?

MECHANIC MATING

TRY NOT TO BE A TOTAL SPANNER.

- I'd love to check out your undercarriage.

- Can you set up my GPS system? I need directions to your heart.

- Is your battery dead? Cause I'd love to jump you.

- I need some coolant, because you've got my engine overheating.

- Do you mind if I check out your exhaust pipe?

- My nuts are made of titanium.

- Nice headlights.

- I will brake, shock, and exhaust you!

PEN PALS

WHEN WRITERS WANT TO END A SENTENCE WITH A PROPOSITION.

- I'm not possessive, but I still want you to be mine.

- I know the difference between 'less' and 'fewer', but don't worry, you won't have to ask me for either of them.

- Let's pretend we're an infinitive so we can never be split.

- I am your subject. Will you be my predicate?

- I'm no adjective; I would never want to modify you.

- Can I call you 'whom'? Because you're the object of my affections.

- After tonight, I guarantee you'll never forget the difference between 'lie' and 'lay'.

- I know that yes means yes. I know that no means no. I even know what 'nor' means.

- Do you like interjections? YES? NO! GOOD!

- Are you a verb? Because you look a little tense, but I can put you in the mood.

WANDERLUST

WHEN YOU TRAVEL, BE IT FOR WORK
OR ON HOLIDAY, THE PROSPECTS ARE
THERE TO MEET MANY NEW PEOPLE
AND TRY A CHAT-UP LINE OR TWO.

If a line works well, the internet is a great way to keep in touch until you can both be in the same part of the world again. If you fail with everyone you encounter, at least you're leaving town by the end of the week.

It can be a gamble though. Trying a chat-up line at the beginning of a long-haul flight could mean the next hours are packed with flirtatious fun. Or if your line does not land well, you may be surprised to find out who the air marshal is.

AIRPORT ARMOUR

CHECKING THEM OUT WHILE CHECKING IN.

- Are you ready to board?

- Want to stamp my passport?

- What's your address? I need to write it on my luggage tag in case my bags get lost and they need to find me.

- Are you a customs agent? Because I'd like to declare my love for you.

- You aren't allowed on the plane 'cause you da bomb, Baby.

- If you've finished checking my bag, there's one more set of underwear to go through.

- Is that a 747 or my heart taking off?

- You've set off my babe detector and I'm afraid I'm going to have to scan you with my wand.

IN-FLIGHT SERVICE

IT'S NOT JUST THE SEAT IN THE UPRIGHT POSITION.

- I hear the Mile High Club is accepting members, shall we join?

- It's not just the towels that are hot in first class.

- According to the lights, the bathroom is unoccupied right now.

- Are you ready for take-off?

- I get nervous when I fly – do you mind if I hold your hand?

- I'd love to be your final destination.

- It's always a first-class trip with me.

- You don't need a seat cushion as a flotation device.

- Which language would you like me to ask you out in?

- I know a great remedy for jet lag.

- I wouldn't complain about a layover with you.

FINAL DESTINATION

NEVER GET BORED ABROAD.

- Everything has been so wonderful since you Cayman to my life.

- Are you from Kingston? Because Jamaican me crazy.

- I just want you to know: I think you're El Salvadorable.

- Are you from Prague? Because I can't help but Czech you out.

- Any chance I could Dubai you dinner tonight?

- I Ecuador you.

- Are you sure you're not a tower? Because Eiffel for you.

- Are you from Paris? Because you're driving me in-Seine.

- I'm Havana dream about you.

- Are you heading to India? Because I'd Goa anywhere with you.

- The way our eyes were Interlaken, I knew you were the one.

ARE YOU IRISH?
BECAUSE YOU'RE
DUBLIN MY
HEART RATE.

ARE YOU
AUSTRALIAN?
BECAUSE YOU
MEET ALL OF MY
KOALA-FICATIONS.

ARE YOU FROM
SOUTH KOREA?
BECAUSE I KNOW
YOU'RE MY
SEOUL-MATE.

TOURIST TALENT

WHEN YOU'RE HOLIDAY-MAKING OUT.

- I'm new in town. Where's good for breakfast?

- There isn't a word in my phrase book for how good you look.

- Could you give me directions to wherever you're going?

- It's my last night here. Do you want to give me a reason to come back?

- You're the only sight I want to see today.

- I'd like to go for a walking tour of your heart.

- How do I get visa approval to visit you?

- We don't need a translator because I speak the language of love.

PULLING PASSENGERS

ISN'T A TRAIN GOING INTO A TUNNEL A METAPHOR FOR SOMETHING?

- The next stop's mine, pull this cord.

- I love the way you grip that pole.

- Is there a doctor on board? Because my bare left ring finger is caught in the door.

- Mind if I sit on your lap? My knees are suddenly weak.

- I may have been waiting for this train for 20 minutes, but I've been waiting for you my whole life.

- No track work needed here, you're in fine shape.

- Can you tell me which bus I need to get to the high street? And your phone number in case I get lost?

- At least we've started on the right track.

YOU DO KNOW HOW TO INFLATE YOUR RAFT, DON'T YOU? JUST PUT YOUR LIPS TOGETHER AND BLOW.

BEACH BALLS

**CAREFUL, SAND GETS EVERYWHERE.
EVERYWHERE.**

- Do you have sunburn, or are you always this hot?

- You hear that? The ocean wants you to join me for a drink.

- Is your name Summer? Cause you are hot!

- How was your last skinny dip? I bet I can make your next one better.

- I've got a few ideas for that surfboard leash.

- Can you call a lifeguard? Because I'm drowning in your eyes...

- I'd swim across the ocean just to see you smile.

- I could put some motion in your ocean.

- I must be lost... I thought paradise was further south.

- I seem to have sand in my bathing suit, wanna get it out?

- I was looking for treasure and I think I found some.

- I'm a Love Pirate, and I'm here for your booty! AAAARRRRRR!

TAXI DRIVERS

YOU LOOKING AT ME?

- This cab is nearly as dirty as me.
- Do you like what you see in the rear view mirror?
- You make my wheels turn.
- I hope your brakes can handle these curves.
- I bet my exhaust is louder than you.
- This back seat is very lonely.
- Do you want to earn a bigger tip?
- You drive me crazy.
- Two lovely airbags and a fantastic bumper.

POOLSIDE PASSIONS

A WORD OF WARNING – SHRINKAGE.

- Is that snorkel bigger than most?

- People tell me I have a good breaststroke, but I'd say I'm a pretty good swimmer too.

- That sure is a lovely set of lungs you are wearing today.

- I'm drowning in your eyes and I need mouth to mouth now!

- You should go in the water, because you're on fire!

- I wish I'd brought my towel, can I share yours?

- You're like the anti-fog spray for my goggles, you just brighten up my day.

- Are you the deep end? Because I'm ready to dive right in.

- If someone throws sharks in the water, I'll save you first.

APRÈS-SKI

PICK THE WRONG LINE AND IT'S DOWNHILL ALL THE WAY.

- I think I must have got on the wrong chairlift... I didn't mean to go straight to heaven!

- You're like gluhwein: a little bit sweet and incredibly hot.

- I'm wearing knee pads and I'm not afraid to use them.

- I can clear snow off my goggles with my tongue.

- Under this helmet and these goggles I look just like Brad Pitt/Angelina Jolie. Honest.

- If your hands are cold, it's warm under my thigh vents.

- Get off the mountain – you're so hot you're melting all the snow!

- The snow may be soft, but I'm not.

HOTEL HOOK-UPS

OH COME ON, GET A ROOM.

- Have you checked in yet? Because I've been checking you out for hours.

- I'm on the floor below you. I'm having a party and I want to invite your pants to come on down.

- I'd cuddle you all morning, checkout times be damned.

- If you were a hotel, I'd give you five stars.

- I brought extra earplugs for the people in the next room.

- How many rewards points do I need for a night with you?

- I'd like to call you in for a little 'room service'.

BONDING WITH BACKPACKERS

BECAUSE THERE IS A REASON IT'S CALLED A RUCKSACK.

- I'd like to explore your hidden gems.

- I don't want to visit the touristy places. Wherever you go is beautiful enough for me.

- You might just have what it takes to turn this nomad into a Bedouin.

- Good thing I've got travel insurance, because things are about to get wild.

- Up for a little adventure?

- There's one thing I pack that isn't travel size. Wanna see?

- See if you can find my money belt.

- Shall we test the hostel's noise policy?

- This wouldn't feel like a Lonely Planet if I were with you.

- You just went straight to the top of my bucket list.

BARFLY

A FEW DRINKS WILL HELP. A FEW MORE MIGHT NOT.

- Do you believe in love at first sight or do I pass by you again?

- Don't you know me from somewhere?

- If this bar is a meat market, you must be the prime rib.

- Excuse me, is that your perfume that you are wearing?

- Do you mind if I stare at you up close instead of from across the room?

- Is that suit/dress felt? Would you like it to be?

- You should stop drinking, because you're driving me home.

- Would you like to meet my bed? It would like to meet you.

THE
APPROACH

YOU MAY NOT REALISE HOW MUCH
THE CHAT-UP LINE YOU CHOOSE SAYS
ABOUT YOU. FIRSTLY, IT SAYS SOMETHING
ABOUT YOUR CHARACTER. ARE YOU
THE BOLD, BRASH TYPE? ARE YOU MORE
SHY AND ENIGMATIC? OR ARE YOU A
CREEPY STALKER BEGGING FOR
A RESTRAINING ORDER?

Secondly, it can often say something about your intentions. By using a chat-up line in the first place, it's clear what's on your mind. But a light-hearted request for a phone number or a dance may be more likely to garner a 'Yes' than a barely disguised plea for sex.

Just be sure that your choice does suit who you are – it's a shame if the charm ebbs away within minutes. And if you do pick someone up with a truly creepy line, imagine how disappointed they would be if you don't have a sack and a van after all.

NUMBER'S UP

WHAT WILL YOU DO WITH THOSE DIGITS?

- I was blinded by your beauty, so I'm going to need your name and number for insurance purposes.

- Do you have the time? The time to write down your number?

- Hi, I'm writing a phone book. I need your number or I'll get fired.

- There's something wrong with my mobile. It's just that your number isn't in it.

- I'm no mathematician, but I'm pretty good with numbers. Tell you what, give me yours and watch what I can do with it.

- Can I even get a fake number?

- Pardon me, I seem to have lost my phone number, could I borrow yours?

- I'm trying to memorise all the phone numbers in the world. The only one I don't know is yours.

- So, tell me about yourself – your dreams, your ambitions, your phone number.

- They say dating is a numbers game... so can I get your number?

BIG YOURSELF UP

NO ONE LIKES A LOSER.

- Sweet, intelligent, spontaneous, good-looking, nice friends, charming, funny. Enough about me, how about you?

- Do you have a boyfriend? Would you like a better one?

- When I woke up this morning I had no plans to be this sexy, but hey.

- I really lack the words to compliment myself today.

- I hate when I am about to hug someone really sexy and my face hits the mirror.

- The last time I had sex it was so good that even the neighbours had a cigarette.

- Don't hate me because I'm beautiful. Hate me because your boyfriend thinks so.

- Wow, your eyes are like my Porsche.

- I'm not really this tall. I'm just sitting on my wallet.

PUT YOURSELF DOWN

NO ONE LIKES A BOASTER.

– I've left my credit card behind the bar. Drink until I'm really good looking, then come and talk to me.

– You take away the looks, money, intelligence, charm and success and there's no real difference between me and Johnny Depp.

– Help the homeless. Take me home with you.

– Each one of my 27 personalities found you cute.

– My mother would approve of you, which is good, since I still live with her.

– I'm looking for baggage that goes with mine.

– Do you have a job? I need a woman who can support me while I play video games all day.

– Does this mean I won't be a virgin by the end of the week?

– What's a nice girl like you doing talking to a loser like me?

– Therapy has been boring recently. Do you want to give me something to talk about?

- You're gorgeous so I'm sure you've heard all the good Cheeky Chat-Up Lines before. Why don't you just tell me the ones that worked and we'll get this out of the way?

- I'm sorry, I have amnesia. Do I come here often?

TRULY CHEEKY

NOT FOR THE FAINTHEARTED.

- Bond. James Bond.

- Yes, you look like my second wife! And I've only been married once!

- My bedroom has a very interesting ceiling.

- Pick a number between 1 and 10. Oh, sorry, you lose. Now take off your clothes.

- Scientists call me a medical miracle.

- So, come back to my place, and if you don't like it I swear I'll give you a full refund.

- For my next trick I need a condom and a volunteer...

- Do you like one-night stands? I hate them too. I've got all weekend.

PLAIN CREEPY

WHEN DOES IT STOP BEING A CHAT-UP LINE AND START BECOMING A THREAT?

- In my nursing class we just learned how to bathe people. Can I practise on you?

- Did you know that your body is made up of 70% water? And now I'm thirsty.

- I run faster horny than you do scared.

- Does this rag smell like chloroform to you?

- Anyone have any sex lying around they're not using I could borrow?

- If I followed you home, would you keep me?

- I can't make you want me. All I can do is stalk you and hope you give in.

- Roses are red, violets are blue, I have a gun, get in the car.

- I wanna live in your socks so I can be with you every step of the way.

LET'S DANCE

MAKE SURE YOUR MOVES ARE AS GOOD AS THE LINE.

- \<Hold out hand\> Hey, will you hold this while I head for the dance floor?

- You see my friends over there? They want to know if you'd like to dance with me.

- Are you a magnet? Cause you attracted me from across the dancefloor.

- Dancing without you would be like a broken pencil – pointless.

- I'm not a hipster, but I can make your hips stir.

- Do you think we would look cute dancing together? I think we should find out.

- Are you an alien? Because I've got a feeling that dancing with you will be like nothing else on earth.

- I've just discovered that my feet won't dance by themselves. Please help!

- Would you like to dance?

CAST A NET ON THE 'NET

ALWAYS ASK FOR A PICTURE POSING WITH A COPY OF TODAY'S NEWSPAPER.

- In my mind, you're always trending.

- It would take me much more than 140 characters to fully express how beautiful you are.

- I usually don't follow someone on the first night, but for you I'll make an exception.

- Every breath you take... every tweet you make... I'll be following you.

- If you were a tweet, you'd be my only favourite.

- Hey gorgeous, will you be my Tinderella?

- You must be a small amount of red phosphorus and I must be a tiny wooden stick, because we're a match.

- Do you believe in love at first swipe?

- Can we be Facebook friends with benefits?

- If I poke you will you poke me back?

- Can I call you my tweet heart?

GEEKY CHEEK

IF THEY UNDERSTAND THE LINE AT ALL, THEN THERE'S HOPE.

- You're more special than relativity.

- Wanna expand my polynomial?

- Your smile must be a black hole – nothing can escape its pull.

- Are you the square root of –1? Because you can't be real.

- Are you made of copper and tellurium? Because you're CuTe.

- Forget hydrogen, you're my number one element.

- You're sweeter than 3.141592.

- I've got my ion you, baby!

PRINCE CHARMING

THERE'S A FINE LINE BETWEEN CHARM AND CHEESE.

- Hey, don't I know you? Yeah, you're the girl with the beautiful smile.

- If I had a rose for every time I thought of you, I would be walking through my garden forever.

- Excuse me miss, can I have the time? I'd check my watch but I can't take my eyes off you.

- I didn't know angels could fly so low.

- There are only two beautiful girls in the world, and you are both of them.

- You're so beautiful you made me forget my pickup line.

- I'm sorry I wasn't part of your past. Can I make it up by being in your future?

- I wish I was one of your tears, so I could be born in your eye, run down your cheek, and die on your lips.

- I thought happiness started with an H. Why does mine start with U?

- Come live in my heart, and pay no rent.

EXCUSE ME, I THINK YOU HAVE SOMETHING IN YOUR EYE. OH WAIT, IT'S JUST A SPARKLE.

WHEN I FIRST SAW YOU I LOOKED FOR A SIGNATURE, BECAUSE EVERY MASTERPIECE HAS ONE.

I DON'T KNOW IF YOU'RE BEAUTIFUL, I HAVEN'T GOT PAST YOUR EYES YET.

THE CLASSICS

THESE LINES WENT INTO THE ARK TWO BY TWO.

- Are your feet tired? You've been running around my mind all day.

- Did it hurt? When you fell from heaven.

- Do you know what'd look good on you? Me.

- How do you like your eggs cooked? I just wanted to know what to make for your breakfast.

- If I told you that you had a great body, would you hold it against me?

- That dress looks great on you, but it would look better on my bedroom floor.

- If I could rearrange the alphabet I'd put U and I together.

- Get your coat, you've pulled.

- Do you know what my shirt is made of? Boyfriend material.

GETTING FRESH

WHEN SUBTLETY IS NOT YOUR STRONG POINT.

- I spent a fortune on Viagra today, only to come here and see you and find out that I don't need it after all.

- Wanna get together and test the spring potential of my mattress?

- I have a six inch tongue and I can breathe through my ears.

- OH GOD! OH GOD! Just practising.

- Trust me. It will only seem kinky the first time.

- I've got a condom with your name on it.

- Virginity is curable.

- Let's play 'Titanic'. When I say 'Iceberg!' you go down.

WELL SEASONED

THE NATURAL WORLD KNOWS HOW
TO ADAPT OVER THE COURSE OF A YEAR.
MAMMALS REPLACE THEIR FUR, BIRDS
REPLACE THEIR FEATHERS AND TREES
REPLACE THEIR LEAVES. AND, IF YOU PICK
THE RIGHT MOMENT, YOU CAN REPLACE
YOUR STATUS OF 'SINGLE' WITH
'IN A RELATIONSHIP'.

Over 365 days the weather changes outside, as do the events going on inside. That is unless you live a simple life, alone, in the desert. In which case, are you sure you're not trying to chat up a palm tree?

Back in civilisation, a good chat-up line should sit well with its environment. And if you deliver it well, you may sit well with the recipient.

SUMMER DAZE

JUST ABOUT ANY REFERENCE TO 'HOT' WILL DO.

- As they say, if you can't take the heat, get out of your clothes.

- Just like the sun, I go down every night.

- Are you related to the sun? Because running into you just brightened up my day.

- Don't worry about the parasol. There's nothing shady about me.

- How far back does your beach chair go?

- Do you want to help test my new hammock?

- Did the sun come out or did you just smile at me?

- Can I swim in your eyes on a hot summer day?

- I'll show you my tan lines if you show me yours.

STORMY WEATHER

WHEN THEY'VE JUST CHANGED THE FORECAST TO SEXY.

- The storm might knock out the power, but your eyes have all the electricity I need.

- If a kiss was a raindrop I would send you a thunderstorm!

- There's a hurricane coming. Evacuate your clothes immediately.

- Want to see my lightning rod?

- I figured out why the sky was grey today. All the blue is in your eyes.

- Is there a rainbow today? Because I just found the treasure.

THAT'S NOT A CANDY CANE IN MY POCKET, I'M VERY PLEASED TO SEE YOU.

CHRISTMAS STALKING

WHEN YOU'RE LOOKING THROUGH MORE WINDOWS THAN AN ADVENT CALENDAR.

- Can I have your picture so I can show Santa what I want for Christmas?

- Shouldn't you be on top of the tree, Angel?

- Let's both be naughty this year and save Santa the trip.

- Wanna meet Santa's little helper?

- I can tell you're quite the elf-a male.

- Interested in seeing the North Pole?

- If I was the Grinch, I wouldn't steal Christmas. I'd steal you.

- You are the reason Santa even has a naughty list.

- How about I slip down your chimney, at half past midnight?

- I'd love to show you the toys the elves make for adults.

- Santa's lap isn't the only place wishes come true.

A WINTER'S TAIL

JACKET ON OR JACKET OFF?

- Baby, you're so hot I only need four layers.

- Do you want to see my snowballs?

- I didn't think I was a snowman, but you just made my heart melt.

- I like your earmuffs. Maybe my flatmate can borrow them when we're back at mine later.

- I lost my scarf, mind if I wrap your legs around me instead?

- My icicles are getting longer.

- I'd like to hiber-mate with you.

- Black ice isn't the only thing I'm falling for.

- Do I have pneumonia? Because you're giving me chills.

- I'm wearing a lot of layers – want to watch me undress for twelve minutes?

NEW YEAR KNOCK-OUTS

OUT WITH THE OLD, IN WITH THE NEW.

- Can I be your first mistake of the year?

- I hear your resolution is to meet the man of your dreams. Well, I'm here.

- I've heard it's bad luck not to kiss someone at midnight.

- Let's ring in the new year with a bang!

- I've got a party hat. Wanna be a noisemaker?

- Put that glass down – I can think of better places to pour champagne.

HALLOWEEN HONEYS

MAKE SURE YOU'RE THE ONE TO SPOOK FIRST.

- That's a nice witch costume, but you won't be needing the broom anymore, because you've already swept me off my feet.

- What's a nice ghoul like you doing in a crypt like this?

- You're the most boo-tiful ghost I've seen all night!

- I would totally carve your pumpkin.

- If I were a zombie, I'd eat you first.

- You are dead sexy.

- I wanna bob for your apples.

- I'm no vampire but I'm fine with getting no sleep and biting your neck all night.

- I want to ask you out, but I've got butterflies in my stomach. And worms. And maggots...

- Why'd you dress up as a princess, when you could have simply come in plain clothes as 'the most beautiful girl at the Halloween party'?

- You're decomposing in all the right places.

- That skeleton over there said he'd get your number for me, but he didn't have the guts, so here I am.

- Do you want to find out what I turn into at midnight?

BE MY VALENTINE

AT LEAST YOU MIGHT NOT END THE DAY SINGLE.

- I'm sorry I didn't get you a box of chocolates for Valentine's Day, but if you want something sweet I'm right here.

- Once you go Cupid, the rest are just stupid.

- When I look at you, I see more stars than there are in your favourite rom-com.

- Coffee, tea or love potion number 9?

- Want to go and judge couples based on their body language with me?

- Do you believe in love at first sight, or should I tell Cupid to shoot you with that arrow one more time?

- Like a box of chocolates, I want to take your top off.

EASTER ENGAGEMENTS

WHEN YOU'RE ON IT LIKE AN EASTER BONNET.

- You think those eggs are big?

- Shall we go at it like bunnies?

- I came here looking for a little tail.

- You can be my chocolate bunny. I'll start by nibbling on your ears and save your behind for last.

- Let's make it a Great Friday.

- Hi, I'm the Easter Bunny and I don't care if you are naughty or nice!

- I'm on a hunt – for your number.

- You're not just somebunny, you're my bunny.

- You put the cream in my eggs.

HAPPY BIRTHDAY TO YOU

WISHING YOU MANY HAPPY RETURNS.

- Want to see my birthday suit?

- The birthday party might be over, but the real party is about to start.

- Birthday sex?

- I know your birthday is only once a year but you're so special it should be every day.

- How about we take this cake to bed and you make a wish?

- All you have to do is unwrap your present – me.

- Can I blow your candle?

- How do you expect me to remember your birthday, when you never look any older?

- I wanted to send you something sexy for your birthday, but the postman made me get out of the postbox.

- Well, I'm here. What are your next two wishes?

HERE COMES THE BRIDE

WHERE STRONG EMOTIONS MEET FREE BOOZE.

- You don't need to catch the bouquet to get lucky.

- I just want to dunk your head under that chocolate fountain and go to town on your face.

- I'd love to buy you a drink from the free bar.

- If you're the bride, congratulations. If not, can I have your number?

- You can make me the third happiest person in the room.

- We might as well get to know one another. We'll probably be seeing each other at baby showers and anniversary parties.

- Wouldn't we look cute on a wedding cake together?

- You're so beautiful I'd marry your brother just to get into your family.

- I've got a bottle of champagne and the keys to an empty limo with an incredibly spacious back seat.

FANCY FANCY DRESS

WHAT'S BEHIND THE MASK?

- Me skull and crossbones aren't the only thing I plan on raisin' tonight.

- They call me the Man of Steel. Well, at least, parts of me.

- Let me Slytherin your Griffendoor.

- I'll tie you up with my lasso of truth and show how an Amazon fights.

- Are you Katniss Everdeen? Because you've got my District in an uprising.

- I could get you undressed in less than 12 parsecs.

- You must be Cinderella, because I see that dress disappearing by midnight.

- Ropes, spurs, leather, chaps – even if I weren't a cowboy, you know it's going to be a good time.

- This is not a costume – I am Batman.

- I couldn't find a costume in time, so I came as your next boyfriend.

- Forget about Spiderman, Superman, and Iron Man. I'll be your man.

ALLSORTS

SO YOU SEE SOMEONE YOU WANT
TO APPROACH. BUT IT'S NO PARTICULAR
TIME OF YEAR AND YOU DON'T KNOW
THEIR JOB OR WHAT INTERESTS THEM.
THAT MEANS THAT SPECIFICS ARE OUT –
YOU CAN'T OPEN WITH A CHAT-UP LINE
ABOUT ACCOUNTANCY, WINTER
WEATHER AND FOOTBALL.*

Essentially, you have no hook for your line. But don't worry – you're not sunk yet.

There are plenty of lines that aren't shackled with any reference to time, place or other particulars. Consider this last collection as your all-purpose chat-up multi-tool. Or actually carry a multi-tool with you instead so you can make an innuendo about what's in your pocket.**

*Just in case you ever do need it – 'I'll make it my goal to warm up your frozen assets'.

**You can work that one out yourself.

IF YOU...

WHEN YOU NEED A FRAME OF REFERENCE. OR A PUN.

- If you were a potato, you'd be a sweet one.

- If you were a vegetable, you'd be a cute-cumber.

- If you were a chicken, you'd be impeccable.

- If you were a steak, you'd be well done.

- If you were finer, you'd be China.

- If you were a dinosaur, you'd be a gorgeousaurus.

- If you were a fruit, you'd be a fineapple.

- If you were a tree, you'd be an evergreen, because I bet you look this good all year round.

- If you were words on a page, you'd be hard to read as your print would be so fine.

- If you were an angle, you'd be acute one.

- If you were a laser gun, you'd be set on stunning.

WHAT ARE YOU SUGGESTING?

LIKE WE DON'T KNOW...

- How about having breakfast in bed with me?

- Look at my lips and your lips. They want to massage each other.

- Picture this: you, me, bubble bath, and a bottle of champagne.

- I need someone really bad. Are you really bad?

- Smile. It's the second best thing you can do with your lips.

- So, what are the chances that we can engage in anything more than just conversation?

- You can stay, but your clothes must go.

- You, me, handcuffs, and whipped cream: interested?

- Nice suit. Can I talk you out of it?

- Is my underwear showing? Would you like it to?

- Excuse me, I'm a little short on cash. Mind if we share a cab home?

ARE YOU MY APPENDIX? BECAUSE I HAVE A FUNNY FEELING IN MY STOMACH THAT MAKES ME FEEL LIKE I SHOULD TAKE YOU OUT.

WHAT ARE YOU?

DON'T TRY MORE THAN ONE OF THESE IN THE SAME CONVERSATION – YOU'LL JUST LOOK CONFUSED.

- Are you a magician? Because whenever I look at you, everyone else disappears.

- Are you an interior decorator? Because when I saw you, the entire room became beautiful.

- Are you a camera? Because every time I look at you, I smile.

- Are you a banana? Because I find you a-peeling.

- Are you a parking ticket? Because you've got fine written all over you.

- Are you religious? Because you're the answer to all my prayers.

- Are you a broom? Because you just swept me off my feet.

- Are you a god? Because I want to kneel before you.

- Are you a ninja? Because you snuck into my heart.

- Are you a high jumper? Because you raise my bar.

QUESTION TIME

QUESTIONS THAT DEMAND ANSWERS.

- Are you going to kiss me or do I have to lie to my diary?

- Can I add a branch to your family tree?

- If nothing lasts forever, will you be my nothing?

- Are you a virgin? Prove it!

- Do you believe in the hereafter? Then you know what I'm here after.

- Can I follow you home? Because my parents always told me to follow my dreams.

- Do you know karate? Because your body is really kickin'.

- Do you like jigsaw puzzles? Let's go to my room and put our pieces together.

- Have you ever played 'Spank the brunette'? Want to try?

- Have you ever played leap frog naked?

- Are you taking any applications for a boyfriend?

- If I were to ask you out on a date, would your answer be the same as the answer to this question?

HELLO, ARE YOU MARRIED? YES? WELL I DIDN'T HEAR YOU SAY 'HAPPILY'.

DO YOU REMEMBER ME? OH THAT'S RIGHT, WE'VE ONLY MET IN MY DREAMS.

IF I GAVE YOU A SEXY NEGLIGEE, WOULD THERE BE ANYTHING IN IT FOR ME?

BOLD AS
YOU LIKE

LET'S NOT BE SHEEPISH.

- I like your last name. Can I have it?

- Come on. We're leaving.

- Hey there. I'm Mr Right... someone said you were looking for me.

- Can you believe that just a few hours ago we'd never even been to bed together?

- Is that a mirror in your pocket? Because I can see myself in your pants.

- Are you busy tonight at 3 a.m.?

- I'm on top of things. Would you like to be one of them?

- Do I know you? Because you look a lot like my next girlfriend.

- Oh all right, I'll stay the night.

AT IT LIKE ANIMALS

TWO LEGS GOOD, ALL FOURS BETTER.

- Hey, kitten. How about spending some of your nine lives with me?

- Are you a sheep? Because your body is unbaaaaalievable.

- Hi, can I domesticate you?

- Are you a cat? Because you're purrrrrrfect.

- I bet you're like a butterfly, pretty to see but hard to catch!

- I heard that rabbits can make 150 babies a year. How many do you think we can make in an hour?

- Do you like whales? How about a hump-back at my place?

- I've been thinking about you owl night long.

- We can play zoo and you can tame my monkey.

ANY TIME, ANY PLACE, ANY WHERE

EXCEPT, PERHAPS, A FUNERAL.

- I usually go for 8's but I guess I'll settle for a 10.

- I think I could fall madly in bed with you.

- You could make a glass eye cry...

- Can I borrow your phone? Because my mum told me to call home when I fell in love.

- Can I see that label? I just wanted to know if you were made in heaven.

- You're single. I'm single. Coincidence? I think not.

- I actually fell for you before I even realised I did.

- Sorry. I can't think of a good ice-breaker. Can you?

- Apart from being sexy, what do you do for a living?

- I was feeling a little off today, but you definitely turned me on.

- I'm sorry, I don't think we've met. I wouldn't forget a pretty face like that.

- My friend thinks you're kinda cute, but I don't... I think you're absolutely gorgeous!

- I wish I had double vision, so I could see you twice.

- Your hand looks heavy. Let me hold it for you.

- Even if there wasn't gravity on earth, I'd still fall for you.

- If you're going to regret this in the morning, we can sleep in until the afternoon.

- Should I smile because we are friends, or cry because I know that is all we will ever be?

- Are you an aspirin? Because I'd like to take you every 4 to 6 hours.

- Be unique and different, just say yes.

- Love is the answer... but while you're waiting for the answer, sex raises some pretty good questions.

- Do you have bones? Then we already have 207 things in common.

- I know 'hello' in six different languages. Which one do you want me to use in the morning?

LAST
RESORT

**THIS SECTION IS FOR REFERENCE
PURPOSES ONLY – THEY WILL NEVER WORK.**

- You're like a car accident, because I just can't look away.

- Just where do those legs of yours end?

- I've fallen for you like a blind roofer.

- You breathe oxygen? We have so much in common.

- Girl, you got more legs than a bucket of chicken.

- Your eyes are as blue as the water in my toilet.

- You're so hot you made fire jealous.

- Hi. You'll do.